Mind Matters: Nurturing Mental Health and 20 Ways to Improve It

Marquise The Coach

Published by Marquise The Coach, 2024.

While every precaution has been taken in the preparation of this book, the publisher assumes no responsibility for errors or omissions, or for damages resulting from the use of the information contained herein.

MIND MATTERS: NURTURING MENTAL HEALTH AND 20 WAYS TO IMPROVE IT

First edition. March 15, 2024.

ISBN: 979-8224701742

Written by Marquise The Coach.

Table of Contents

I want to thank my first English teacher at my college, Theresa Walsh, for inspiring me to become a better writer and giving me more confidence in my writing skills.

Mind Matters: Nurturing Mental Health and 20 Ways to Improve It

Chapter 1: Understanding Mental Health

In this chapter, we will look at the concept of mental health and its importance in our lives. We will look at many areas of mental health, common mental health illnesses, and the significant influence they can have on our general well-being. Understanding the importance of mental health allows us to begin prioritizing and nurturing it more efficiently.

Defining mental health and its significance

Mental health is a multifaceted concept that encompasses our emotional, psychological, and social well-being. It is not a static state but a continuum that fluctuates throughout our lives. Just as we prioritize our physical health, it is equally important to prioritize our mental health.

At its core, mental health involves how we think, feel, and behave. It influences our perception of ourselves, others, and the world around us. A positive mental health state allows us to navigate life's challenges, build resilience, and maintain a sense of well-being. It enables us to cope with stress, form meaningful relationships, and make informed decisions.

The absence of mental illness does not solely determine mental health. It is a holistic state that encompasses various factors, including emotional well-being, cognitive functioning, and social interactions. It involves having a positive sense of self, being able to manage emotions effectively, and maintaining healthy relationships.

When our mental health is compromised, it can have a profound impact on our daily lives. Mental health disorders can manifest in various ways, such as anxiety, depression, mood swings, or difficulty concentrating. These disorders can disrupt our ability to function optimally, affecting our work, relationships, and overall quality of life.

It is important to recognize that mental health is influenced by a combination of genetic, biological, environmental, and social factors. Each individual's experience of mental health is unique, and it is essential to approach it with empathy and understanding.

Promoting mental health involves taking proactive steps to maintain and enhance our well-being. This includes engaging in self-care activities, seeking support when needed, and adopting healthy coping mechanisms. It also involves challenging societal stigmas not only surrounding mental health and promoting open conversations about mental well-being.

By understanding and prioritizing mental health, we can create a foundation for overall well-being. It allows us to cultivate self-awareness, develop emotional intelligence, and build resilience. Nurturing our mental health benefits us as individuals but also contributes to healthier communities and a more compassionate society.

In the following chapters, we will explore practical strategies and techniques to improve mental health. These strategies will empower individuals to take control of their mental well-being and lead happier, more fulfilling lives. Remember, mental health is an essential aspect of our overall well-being, and investing in it is a worthwhile endeavor.

The Significance of Mental Health

Mental health plays a vital role in our overall well-being and quality of life. It affects every aspect of our daily functioning, including our relationships, work performance, and physical health. Understanding the significance of mental health is crucial for individuals, communities, and society as a whole.

Personal Well-being: Mental health is essential for our well-being. When we prioritize our mental health, we are better equipped to handle life's challenges, manage stress, and maintain a positive outlook.

It allows us to experience a sense of fulfillment, contentment, and happiness in our lives.

Relationships: Mental health significantly impacts our relationships with others. When we are mentally healthy, we are more likely to form and maintain healthy and meaningful connections. We can communicate effectively, empathize with others, and build strong support networks. Conversely, when our mental health is compromised, it can strain relationships, leading to conflicts and misunderstandings.

Work Performance: Mental health has a direct impact on our work performance and productivity. When we are mentally healthy, we can focus, concentrate, and make sound decisions. We are more motivated, creative, and resilient in the face of challenges. On the other hand, poor mental health can lead to decreased productivity, absenteeism, and difficulty meeting deadlines.

Physical Health: Mental health and physical health are closely intertwined. Chronic stress, anxiety, and depression can manifest as physical symptoms, such as headaches, digestive issues, and weakened immune function. Conversely, physical health conditions, such as chronic pain or illness, can have a significant impact on mental well-being. Prioritizing mental health can contribute to better physical health outcomes and overall well-being.

Quality of Life: Mental health is a fundamental component of a high-quality life. When we prioritize our mental well-being, we can experience a greater sense of fulfillment, purpose, and satisfaction. We are more likely to engage in activities that bring us joy, pursue our passions, and maintain a positive outlook on life. Investing in mental health leads to a more balanced and fulfilling existence.

Societal Impact: Mental health is not just an individual concern; it has broader societal implications. When individuals prioritize their mental health, it contributes to healthier communities and a more compassionate society. It reduces the stigma surrounding mental health, promotes empathy and understanding, and encourages open conversations about mental well-being. A mentally healthy society is more inclusive, supportive, and resilient.

Recognizing the significance of mental health empowers individuals to take proactive steps toward nurturing and improving their well-being. It encourages seeking support when needed, practicing self-care, and promoting mental health awareness in our communities. By prioritizing mental health, we can lead happier, more fulfilling lives and contribute to a healthier and more compassionate world.

Common Mental Health Disorders And Their Impact

In this section, we will explore some of the most common mental health disorders that affect individuals worldwide. Understanding these disorders is crucial for promoting empathy, reducing stigma, and providing support to those who may be experiencing them.

Anxiety Disorders: Anxiety disorders are characterized by excessive worry, fear, and apprehension. Generalized Anxiety Disorder (GAD), Panic Disorder, Social Anxiety Disorder, and Specific Phobias are some examples. These disorders can significantly impact daily functioning, leading to avoidance behaviors, difficulty in social situations, and physical symptoms such as rapid heartbeat and shortness of breath.

Depression: Depression is a mood disorder characterized by persistent feelings of sadness, hopelessness, and a loss of interest in activities. It can affect sleep, appetite, energy levels, and concentration. Major Depressive Disorder (MDD) is the most common form of depression, and it can significantly impair an individual's ability to function and enjoy life.

Bipolar Disorder: Bipolar Disorder involves extreme mood swings, ranging from periods of intense mania to episodes of depression. During manic episodes, individuals may experience heightened energy, impulsivity, and grandiose thoughts. Depressive episodes are characterized by feelings of sadness, low energy, and a loss of interest in activities. Bipolar Disorder can have a significant impact on relationships, work, and overall stability.

Schizophrenia: Schizophrenia is a chronic mental disorder that affects a person's perception of reality. It involves a combination of hallucinations, delusions, disorganized thinking, and impaired social functioning. Individuals with schizophrenia may experience difficulties in distinguishing between what is real and what is not, making it challenging to navigate daily life.

Eating Disorders: Eating disorders, such as Anorexia Nervosa, Bulimia Nervosa, and Binge Eating Disorder, involve unhealthy relationships with food and body image. These disorders can lead to severe physical and psychological consequences, including malnutrition, organ damage, and emotional distress. They often require a multidisciplinary approach to treatment and recovery.

It is important to note that mental health disorders are complex and can vary in severity and presentation from person to person. They are not a reflection of personal weakness or character flaws but rather the result of a combination of genetic, biological, environmental, and psychological factors.

Supporting individuals with mental health disorders involves providing empathy, understanding, and access to appropriate resources. It is essential to promote mental health awareness, reduce stigma, and encourage open conversations about mental well-being. Seeking professional help from mental health professionals, such as therapists, psychiatrists, and counselors, is often crucial for diagnosis, treatment, and ongoing support.

The Mind-Body Connection: How mental health affects physical well-being

The mind and body are intricately connected, and the state of our mental health has a significant impact on our physical well-being.

Understanding and nurturing the mind-body connection is crucial for maintaining optimal mental health.

Impact of Mental Health on Physical Health: Chronic stress, anxiety, and depression can manifest as physical symptoms and contribute to the development or exacerbation of physical health conditions. For example, prolonged stress can weaken the immune system, making individuals more susceptible to illnesses. Anxiety and depression can lead to changes in appetite, sleep disturbances, and increased risk of cardiovascular problems. By addressing and managing mental health, we can positively influence our physical health outcomes.

Stress Management Techniques: Stress is a natural response to challenging situations, but chronic stress can have detrimental effects on mental and physical health. Engaging in stress management techniques is essential for maintaining a healthy mind-body balance. Techniques such as relaxation exercises, deep breathing, mindfulness, and meditation can help reduce stress levels, promote relaxation, and improve overall well-being.

Exercise and Mental Health: Regular physical exercise has been shown to have numerous benefits for mental health. Exercise releases endorphins, which are natural mood-boosting chemicals in the brain. It can reduce symptoms of anxiety and depression, improve sleep quality, and enhance overall cognitive function. Engaging in activities such as walking, jogging, yoga, or dancing can have a positive impact on both mental and physical well-being.

Sleep and Mental Health: Sleep plays a vital role in maintaining good mental health. Lack of sleep or poor sleep quality can contribute to increased stress levels, mood disturbances, and difficulties in cognitive functioning. Establishing a consistent sleep routine, creating a sleep-friendly environment, and practicing relaxation techniques before bed can promote better sleep and support mental well-being.

Nutrition and Mental Health: The food we consume can have a significant impact on our mental health. A balanced diet that includes nutrient-rich foods, such as fruits, vegetables, whole grains, lean proteins, and healthy fats, provides the necessary nutrients for optimal brain function. On the other hand, a diet high in processed foods, sugar, and unhealthy fats can contribute to inflammation and negatively affect mental health. Making conscious choices to prioritize nutritious foods can support both mental and physical well-being.

Substance Abuse and Mental Health: Substance abuse can have severe consequences on mental health. Individuals may turn to substances as a way to cope with emotional pain or to self-medicate symptoms of mental health disorders. However, substance abuse often exacerbates mental health issues and can lead to a vicious cycle of dependency and worsening mental well-being. Seeking professional help and support groups are essential for individuals struggling with substance abuse and mental health disorders.

By recognizing the mind-body connection and implementing strategies to support both mental and physical well-being, we can enhance our overall quality of life. Taking care of our mental health through stress management, exercise, sleep hygiene, nutrition, and avoiding substance abuse can contribute to a healthier and more balanced mind-body state.

Incorporating these practices into our daily lives can help us better manage stress, improve mood, and enhance our overall resilience. By nurturing the mind-body connection, we can create a solid foundation for optimal mental health and well-being.

In this chapter, we have explored the fundamental aspects of mental health and its significance in our lives. We have defined mental health as our emotional, psychological, and social well-being, emphasizing that it is not merely the absence of mental illness but a state of overall well-being. By understanding the importance of mental health, we can begin to prioritize and nurture it effectively.

We have discussed common mental health disorders, including anxiety disorders, depression, bipolar disorder, schizophrenia, and eating disorders. Understanding these disorders is crucial for promoting empathy, reducing stigma, and providing support to those who may be experiencing them. By recognizing that mental health disorders are complex and multifaceted, we can create a more compassionate and inclusive society that supports individuals in their journey toward recovery and well-being.

Furthermore, we have explored the mind-body connection and its profound impact on our overall well-being. Mental health and physical health are closely intertwined, and taking care of our mental well-being positively influences our physical health outcomes. By engaging in stress management techniques, regular exercise, prioritizing sleep, maintaining a balanced diet, and avoiding substance abuse, we can nurture the mind-body connection and enhance our overall quality of life.

Remember, mental health is a journey, and it is important to seek support when needed. Whether it is through professional help, support groups, or trusted individuals in our lives, reaching out for assistance is a sign of strength. Together, we can create a world where mental health is prioritized, stigma is reduced, and individuals are supported in their pursuit of well-being.

Chapter 2: Building Resilience and Emotional Well-being

In this chapter, we will look at the significance of developing resilience and nurturing emotional well-being. Resilience is the ability to recover from hardship, whereas emotional well-being is the efficient understanding and management of our emotions. By honing these talents, we may better handle life's ups and downs and live more rewarding lives.

Knowing how to bounce back from tough situations.

Resilience is an important quality that helps us bounce back from tough times and handle stress and challenges. It's not about avoiding problems or acting like everything is always great. It's about getting stronger and learning how to face challenges and come back even better. Resilience is like a muscle that can get stronger with practice and time.

An important part of being resilient is knowing that everyone faces problems and failures sometimes. Instead of seeing them as impossible problems, we can think of them as chances to get better and learn. Strong people know that bad things don't last forever and they can overcome them.

Resilience means having a positive attitude. This means thinking about what we are good at instead of thinking about what we are not good at. By recognizing what we are good at, we can feel more sure of ourselves and believe that we can handle tough situations. Growing gratitude is also important for having a positive attitude. Pausing to notice the good things in our lives, even when things are hard, can help us see things in a better way and become stronger.

Another important part of being strong is being able to change and adjust to new situations. Life is full of surprises and things we can't predict. It's important to be able to adjust to new situations. Resilient people can adapt and are ready for new opportunities. They welcome change as a chance to grow and are ready to change their plans and strategies when needed.

It is important to have a strong support system to be resilient. Having people you trust like friends, family, or mentors to give you emotional support, advice, and motivation can help when things get tough. When we talk about our problems with others and ask for help, it can help us see things in a new way, find answers, and not feel so lonely.

Finally, being resilient means not giving up and continuing to push forward, even when things get tough. It's about staying determined and not giving up easily. Strong people know that problems and failures don't last forever, and they keep trying to reach their goals even when things are tough.

In short, knowing about resilience means realizing that struggles and obstacles are a normal part of life and seeing them as chances to become stronger. It means thinking positively, being open to change, having a good support system, and never giving up. By learning these skills, we can handle life's challenges better and have happier lives.

Strengthening the Ability to Bounce Back

Building resilience means learning new skills and finding healthy ways to deal with problems so that we can overcome tough times and recover from difficult situations. By actively working on getting stronger, we can become better at handling stress, setbacks, and tough situations. Here are some important ways to build resilience:

Developing a positive outlook: Having a positive attitude can help you become stronger. This means paying attention to the things we are good at, the things we have achieved, and the good parts of our lives. By positively looking at things, we can become more confident and believe in our ability to handle problems. Being thankful can help make us feel more positive. Spend time every day thinking about the things we are thankful for can help us stay positive even when things are tough.

Building Problem-Solving Abilities: Resilient People take the initiative to solve problems. Learning to solve problems means breaking them into smaller parts and coming up with ideas to fix them. It also means being willing to ask for help and advice from people who have experienced similar things. By solving problems, we can become more confident in our ability to handle problems and find solutions that work.

Creating a group of people to support you is very important for being strong. During tough times, having people like friends, family, or mentors who support, guide, and encourage you can help. Talking with others about our problems can help us see things in a new way, figure out what to do, and not feel so lonely. Forming and growing these connections can make us feel like we belong and give us help that makes us stronger.

Taking care of yourself is important for staying strong. It's important to look after our bodies, emotions, and thoughts to stay strong when things get tough. Participating in things that make us happy and relaxed can help reduce stress and improve our overall health. This can mean things like exercising, being in nature, mindfulness or meditation, doing hobbies, or getting help from a professional if you need it.

Being able to change and adapt is important. Resilient people can easily adjust to new situations. They know that life has many unknowns and unexpected things can happen. Being flexible means being open to new ideas, changing our plans when needed, and seeing change as a chance to grow. By being open to change and ready to adjust, we can handle problems more easily and bounce back stronger.

Developing Emotional Intelligence: Emotional intelligence means being able to understand and control our feelings as well as the feelings of people around us. Learning to understand and manage our feelings better can make it easier to deal with tough emotions, talk to others in a good way, and have better relationships. It means knowing our feelings sharing them in a good way, and being understanding of other people's feelings. By learning about our feelings and the feelings of others, we can become better at dealing with problems and challenges.

In short, building resilience means learning how to handle challenges and problems positively. By thinking positively, solving problems, getting help from others, taking care of ourselves, being flexible, and understanding our feelings, we can become stronger and handle difficulties in life better. Becoming resilient takes time and effort but it's worth it. It helps us handle tough situations better.

Dealing with Feelings

Handling emotions well is important for being strong and taking care of our feelings. Feelings are really important in our everyday lives and they can affect how we think, act, and how we feel about ourselves. By understanding our feelings and finding good ways to handle them, we can become stronger and live more stable lives. Here are some important ways to handle your feelings:

Identifying and accepting feelings: The first step in handling emotions is to know and accept them. It's important to understand our feelings and allow ourselves to feel a mix of good and bad emotions. By accepting our feelings without criticizing them, we can start to understand and deal with them better.

Becoming aware of our emotions means figuring out what makes us feel a certain way and why we feel that way. You have to notice how your body feels, what you are thinking, and how you act when you feel different emotions. By paying attention to our feelings, we can understand them better and make smarter decisions about how we react to them.

Dealing with Feelings: It's important to handle your emotions healthily to stay emotionally well. This means finding healthy ways to deal with our feelings, like talking to someone we trust, writing in a journal, or doing something creative. It's important to honestly show your feelings respectfully and think about how they might affect others. We can avoid feeling more upset by sharing our feelings in a good and safe way. Learning to control our feelings is important. It means being able to handle our emotions positively. This means understanding when our emotions are getting too strong and using techniques to make ourselves feel better. Taking deep breaths, doing mindfulness activities, and doing things we enjoy can help us control our feelings. Ignoring or hiding our feelings can harm our well-being in the long run. So, it's important not to do that.

Understanding and caring about other people's feelings and being aware of our own emotions are important for handling emotions well. Empathy means understanding how other people feel and sharing their emotions. It can help us in our relationships with others and make us respond to their feelings with kindness. Understanding and controlling our feelings and knowing how to react to other people's feelings is called emotional intelligence. By understanding and caring about others' feelings and being able to control our own emotions, we can better handle difficult emotional situations and have better relationships.

Getting help from a professional: Sometimes, dealing with your feelings may need a professional's help. If strong feelings are too much or make it hard to do things every day, it can help to talk to a mental health expert. They can help with advice, support, and practical ways to control feelings better.

In summary, controlling your feelings is important for staying strong and taking care of your emotional health. We can get better at handling our feelings by understanding and accepting them, being aware of our emotions, expressing them in a good way, controlling them, understanding how others feel, and getting help when we need it. If we control our feelings, we can become stronger, feel better, and have better relationships with ourselves and others.

Taking care of yourself and dealing with stress.
Taking care of yourself is important for staying strong and keeping your emotions healthy. It means to do things on purpose to make sure we stay healthy in our body, feelings, and mind. Taking care of ourselves can make us feel less stressed, happier, and healthier overall. Here are some important ways to take care of yourself and deal with stress:
Taking care of our body is very important for our health and how we feel. This means doing exercise, eating healthy, and getting enough rest. Taking part in exercise not only makes our bodies healthier but can also make us feel happier and less stressed because it releases chemicals in our brains. Eating healthy food and getting enough sleep gives our bodies the energy and things they need to work their best.
Practicing relaxation techniques can help us deal with stress and feel calm. This can mean doing things like taking deep breaths, relaxing our muscles, or doing things that we enjoy and make us feel calm. Taking breaks during the day to do these things can help us feel better and lower our stress.
Creating boundaries is an important part of taking care of yourself. It means knowing what we can and cannot do and telling others about it. This can mean not doing things that are too much for us, making time for ourselves, and doing things that make us happy and help us relax. Setting boundaries helps us to avoid getting too tired and make sure we can look after ourselves properly.
Practicing mindfulness means being completely focused on what is happening right now, without any opinions or criticism. Mindfulness is about noticing our thoughts, feelings, and sensations with interest and

openness. Doing mindfulness activities like deep breathing or focusing on each part of our body can make us feel less stressed, help us understand ourselves better, and make us feel peaceful. Practicing mindfulness helps us to deal with stress and feel better overall.

Getting help from others is an important part of taking care of yourself. This could involve talking to friends, family, or support groups for help with emotions and advice. You can also ask therapists or counselors for help if you need it. Having people to help us can give us the things we need and keep us feeling positive when things are tough.

Participating in things that make us happy and calm is an important way to take care of ourselves. This can mean things you like to do for fun, being creative, spending time outside, or doing things that help you feel calm, like reading or taking a bath. Making time for things that make us happy and fulfilled helps us feel better and stay positive.

In the end, taking care of yourself and dealing with stress is important for being strong and feeling good emotionally. By taking care of our body, relaxing, setting limits, staying present, getting help, and doing things that make us happy, we can lower stress, feel better, and deal with problems better. Taking care of ourselves is not a bad thing. It's important for our health and helps us be our best in everything we do.

Practicing being aware and focused.

Practicing mindfulness is important for being strong and feeling good emotionally. Mindfulness means being completely focused on what's happening right now and being aware of our thoughts, feelings, and sensations without judging them. By practicing mindfulness every day, we can lower stress, become more aware of ourselves, and feel more peaceful and balanced. Here are a few important ways to practice mindfulness:

Conscious breathing is an easy and helpful way to practice mindfulness. It means paying attention to how we feel when we breathe in and out. By paying attention to the here and now and the feelings of breathing in our body, we can center ourselves and create a feeling of peace. Spending a little time each day doing mindful breathing can make you feel less stressed and boost your well-being.

The body scan is a way to pay close attention to different parts of our body and how they feel. We focus on any sensations or tightness we may feel. This helps us notice how our body feels and can make us less tense and more relaxed. By doing a body scan often, we can become more aware of what our body needs and make a stronger bond between our mind and body.

Eating mindfully means paying close attention to the food we eat, enjoying every bite, and being aware of the taste, feel, and smell of the food. By eating slowly and paying attention to our senses, we can learn to enjoy our food more and have a better way of eating. Being mindful when we eat can help us pay more attention to when we are hungry and when we are full. This can lead to better eating habits and listening to our body's signals.

Being aware of how you move your body can help you be more mindful. Doing activities like yoga, tai chi, or walking while being aware of your movements can help you feel more connected to your mind and body. These practices involve paying attention to how our body feels and moves, while also staying aware and focused. Exercising with careful attention can make you feel calmer, help you move better, and make you stronger. It can also improve your overall health.

Being mindful in communication means paying full attention and being present when talking to others. This means listening with interest and understanding, without being critical or having opinions already formed. We can improve our relationships and understanding by communicating and paying attention to others. This can help us to build stronger connections with others.

Being mindful means paying attention to what we're doing in our everyday tasks, like washing dishes, brushing our teeth, or taking a shower. It's a way to be more aware and present in the moment. When we pay close attention to the things we do and notice the feelings, smells, and movements involved, we can turn regular tasks into chances to be mindful and aware.

In summary, practicing mindfulness is very helpful for building strength and taking care of your emotions. By paying attention to our breathing, checking in with our body, eating slowly and with awareness, moving with purpose, speaking with thoughtfulness, and making mindfulness a part of our everyday routine, we can feel less stressed, more in tune with ourselves, and more peaceful. Mindfulness is not about being perfect or getting rid of all thoughts and distractions. It's about being aware of the present moment without judging it. Regularly practicing mindfulness can help us feel better and handle life's problems more easily.

In this chapter, we have learned about the significance of developing strength and taking care of our emotions. By learning about resilience, we can learn how to bounce back from tough times and become even stronger. Taking control of our feelings and taking care of ourselves helps us feel better emotionally overall. Practicing mindfulness helps us to focus on the present and deal with life's challenges better.

In the next few chapters, we will learn more about ways to become stronger, control our feelings, take care of ourselves, and be more aware of the present moment.

Chapter 3: Building Good Relationships

In mental health, our relationships are the important connections that make up our emotions. The people we are close to, like family, friends, and partners, have a big impact on how we feel. In this chapter, we look at how important it is for people to connect. We explore how these connections help people to be strong, happy, and mentally healthy.

The importance of friends and family in your mental health.

Friends and family are really important for your mental health. Don't underestimate their importance. These relationships are really important for our feelings and help us feel like we belong, and are loved and understood, which is really important for our happiness.

Friends and family are the ones who help us when life gets tough. They give comfort and support when you're having a hard time, by listening, being there for you, and comforting you. When we are dealing with problems in our personal life, work, or relationships, having people we trust to talk to can help us get through tough times.

Friends and family are important for making us feel like we belong and are connected, not just for emotional support. Research has found that being alone and feeling lonely can make your mental health worse, leading to depression and anxiety. On the other hand, having good relationships with others can help protect you from the bad effects of stress, make you more able to handle problems, and make you feel better overall.

Additionally, friends and family give us important chances for happiness, laughter, and to make memories together. Whether we're enjoying special occasions, making happy memories, or just spending time together, these moments help us feel good inside and make our lives better.

But most importantly, friends and family tell us how important we are as people. In a world that focuses on doing well and achieving, these relationships give us love and acceptance no matter what, and make us feel good about who we are and that we deserve love and belonging. Basically, friends and family are not just the people who support us, they are also very important in our lives. Building and taking care of these relationships is not just important for our mental health but also makes our lives better in many ways. Let's appreciate our friendships and family because they are the most important things that support us in life.

Creating and keeping good relationships.

Building and keeping strong connections with others takes planning, hard work, and caring about them. If we want to make good relationships that last a long time, we can use some important ideas. These ideas can help us make new connections and take care of the ones we already have.

Effective communication is very important.

Good communication is very important for a good relationship. It means sharing our thoughts and feelings honestly and also taking the time to really hear and understand what others are saying. By improving how we talk to each other and showing respect, we can solve problems and make our trust and closeness stronger.

Nurture the ability to understand and care about others.

Understanding and sharing the feelings of others is important in good relationships. When we try to understand how other people feel and see things, we can build stronger relationships and show more respect and kindness.

Spend more time with your loved ones.

In today's busy world, it's easy to get too caught up in our schedules and forget to spend time with our family and friends. However, it's important to make a special effort to spend quality time together to help build strong relationships. Spending time together doing things like eating, going for a walk, or just hanging out helps to make relationships stronger.

Express thanks and appreciation.

Showing thanks and being grateful for the people in our lives is a strong way to make good feelings stronger and make our relationships better. Recognizing and celebrating the good things people do helps us to appreciate each other and feel closer.

Be yourself and share your feelings openly.

Being real and open is important for building a real connection with others. When we are honest and open about our thoughts and feelings, it encourages others to do the same. Being open about our feelings and weaknesses makes our relationships stronger and helps us understand each other better.

Learn to forgive and move on.

Disagreements and not understanding can happen in any relationship. Nevertheless, it's important to forgive and forget about past problems so that you can move on and have good relationships. When we forgive and show kindness to others, it helps us heal, grow, and makeup with them in our relationships.

Invest in helping each other grow and support each other.

Good relationships are made by both people helping each other grow and supporting each other. We help each other grow, cheer for each other's accomplishments, and offer support when things get tough. This makes us feel like a team and helps keep our friendships strong.

In short, having good relationships means talking, understanding, spending time together, showing gratitude, being truthful, and forgiving, and helping each other grow. By following these ideas when we talk to others, we can make good relationships that make our lives better and bring happiness to those around us.

Good communication and adequately solving problems.

Effective communication is very important for any good relationship. It helps people share their thoughts, feelings, and needs, and solve problems. Good communication is more than just talking. It also includes listening carefully, understanding others' feelings, and being open and honest in conversations. Good communication and problem-solving skills help make relationships strong and healthy.

Talking openly and honestly: Good communication means sharing your thoughts and feelings without being afraid of being judged or punished. When people can be themselves without worry, it helps build trust, closeness, and understanding in the relationship.

Active Listening: Listening is an important part of communicating well. You need to listen to the person speaking and be fully present in the conversation. Try to understand their point of view without interrupting or making judgments. When people listen carefully to each other, it shows that they care about and understand each other's feelings. This helps them to build a strong bond and show empathy.

Empathy and understanding mean being able to understand and share the feelings of another person. This means understanding and accepting how others feel, and showing that you care and want to help them. By being kind and understanding in conversations, people can make their relationships better and build trust.

Clear and open communication: Good communication needs to be easy to understand and honest when expressing what you are thinking, needing, and expecting. By speaking clearly and directly, people can avoid misunderstandings and disagreements that can cause problems or hard feelings. Transparency helps people be honest and real in their relationships, making it a safe place to talk openly and trust each other.

Dealing with Conflicts: Conflicts happen in all relationships, but how you handle them can make your bond stronger or weaker. Solving problems well means working together to find solutions that everyone can agree on. By being patient, willing to make compromises, and understanding others' feelings, people can work through disagreements positively and come out with a better understanding and respect for each other.

Understanding when there is a problem: Conflict can show up in different ways, like arguments, not understanding each other, or having different beliefs or priorities. Identify problems before they get worse by spotting the signs of conflict early.

Find out why the conflict happened, like if people didn't communicate well, didn't get what they needed, wanted different things, or had problems in the past. Finding the main reasons why the conflict started helps to solve the important issues.

Ways to solve problems and get along with others better.

Encourage people to talk openly and honestly about their problems. Make a place where people can share their thoughts and feelings without being judged or punished.

Active Listening: Pay close attention to the other person's point of view without interrupting or thinking of a response right away. Show you understand and care by acknowledging their feelings and experiences.

Understanding how someone else feels and seeing things from their point of view is called empathy and perspective-taking. It means trying to imagine what it's like to be in their situation and understand their emotions. Fostering empathy helps people understand each other better and bring together different opinions.

Focus on what people want, not their specific demands. Think about what's important to them and what they need. Find things that everyone wants to achieve together to come up with solutions that everyone involved likes.

Thinking together and solving problems: Work together to come up with ideas to solve the conflict and decide if they will work. Approach solving problems by being creative and flexible, and considering different viewpoints and options.

Give up some things and talk to each other to find a solution that everyone can agree on. Find places where you can give up some things without going against the most important beliefs or rules.

Get help from a neutral person like a mediator or facilitator when conflicts are really complicated or hard to solve. They can help make communication and negotiation easier.

Controlling your feelings: Controlling your feelings during arguments by being aware of them and using techniques to handle them well. If you start to feel too emotional, take a break, calm down, and then come back to the conversation.

Prevent fights: Don't make personal attacks, blame others, or get defensive to stop conflicts from getting worse. Keep your attention on the main problem and remember to be positive during the conversation.

Learning to solve problems when people don't agree: Practice and get advice to improve this skill. Think about the fights you've had before and figure out what can be done better. Come up with ways to handle disagreements in a better way next time.

Forgiving and moving on: Try to forgive others and yourself when resolving conflicts. Release the anger and bad feelings you have towards someone to help you feel better and make things right again.

Learning and Growing: See conflicts as chances to learn and grow, both on your own and in your relationships. Think about what we have learned from disagreements and use that knowledge to make our relationships and communication better.

Rebuild trust by taking action to repair any harm done to the relationship during a conflict. Always tell the truth, be trustworthy, and be dependable when you talk to people.

Setting boundaries and being assertive are also important in good communication.

This means respectfully expressing your needs and limits. By clearly telling others what you're comfortable with and what you expect, you create a good way for everyone to interact with each other and show respect in the relationship. In addition, being assertive means people can confidently speak up about what they need and want without being mean or avoiding the issue.

It's really important to have good communication and problem-solving skills to have good and happy relationships. By talking openly, listening well, understanding others, and being honest, people can deal with problems, make relationships stronger, and build a closer and more trusting bond with their partners, family, friends, and co-workers.

As we make friends, we should remember that the people we spend time with can impact how we feel and improve our lives. We can make strong connections that support our mental health by being kind, thoughtful, and communicating openly. Let's remember how important it is to connect with and build relationships with others that make us feel good and support our mental health.

Knowing your own needs, values, and limits is the first step in setting boundaries. Think about what you are okay with and not okay with in different parts of your life like your relationships, job, and personal space.

Be clear when telling others about your limits. Use clear and direct language to say what you want and expect without being unclear or indirectly aggressive.

Consistency: Always stick to your rules by what you say and do. Being consistent helps people trust and respect you in relationships because they know what to expect from you.

Respect Other People's Rules: Just like you want others to respect your rules, try to respect other people's rules too. Look for signs that someone is not comfortable or does not want to do something, and change how you act.

Being flexible means being willing to negotiate and make compromises when needed, even though it's important to have limits. Flexibility helps in making relationships healthy by allowing for mutual understanding and cooperation.

Taking care of yourself is important. Make sure to set boundaries and take care of your well-being. When you feel overwhelmed, it's okay to take a break, turn down extra tasks, or ask for help from people around you. This will help you keep a good balance in your life.

Being assertive means being able to confidently express your thoughts, feelings, and needs while also respecting the rights and opinions of others. It involves standing up for yourself and communicating in a clear and direct manner.

Believing in yourself and respecting yourself makes you confident. Have confidence in yourself and believe in your own importance. Act with self-assurance in your interactions with others.

Being assertive means saying how you feel and what you need truthfully, while also being considerate of others. Use "I" statements to say how you feel and what you have experienced.

Active listening means really paying attention to what other people are saying and showing them that you understand how they feel, even when you want to express your own opinions. Show that you care and try to understand others, so that you can have a good conversation and treat each other with respect.

Body Language: Be aware of how you hold yourself when speaking confidently. Keep looking at the person, sit or stand straight, and use gestures that show you are confident and open.

Setting limits means knowing when to say stop and standing strong when someone tries to control or force you to do something. It's okay to say no when you need to. Don't feel bad or like you have to always please others by saying yes.

Resolving Conflicts: Speaking up and communicating clearly is important for solving problems peacefully. Dealing with disagreements in a team by working together to find a solution that benefits everyone and showing respect for yourself and others.

Practice and getting advice: Like any ability, speaking up for yourself can improve by practicing and learning from others' feedback. Practice difficult situations with others, get help from people you trust, and think about how you talk to keep getting better at standing up for yourself.

Chapter 4: Dealing with Stress and Worry.

In today's fast world, many people feel stressed and anxious, which can affect their mental and emotional health. In this chapter, we will learn about good ways to find what makes us stressed and worried, how to deal with these problems, and how to become stronger when facing tough times.

Recognizing what makes you feel worried and nervous

Identifying what makes you stressed: Knowing the things that make you feel stressed or anxious is the first step to dealing with them better. Identifying what makes you stressed, like deadlines at work, problems in relationships, or money issues, gives you the power to take action to reduce their effects.

Being mindful and reflecting on yourself can help you understand your thoughts, emotions, and physical feelings better, so you can recognize stress and anxiety more easily. By paying attention to their thoughts and feelings and being okay with them, people can understand why they feel stressed and anxious.

Ways to handle stress

Relaxation exercises like deep breathing, muscle relaxation, and guided imagery can help reduce stress and make you feel calm and relaxed. Try doing them every day. These methods make the body feel relaxed and calm, helping to reduce the physical effects of stress and improve health.

Paying close attention and meditating can help with stress and anxiety. By paying attention to the present moment and accepting experiences without judging them, people can feel less stressed, control their emotions better, and find more peace within themselves.

Doing exercises like yoga, tai chi, or aerobic exercise can help reduce stress and anxiety. When you exercise, your body releases chemicals called endorphins. These make you feel happier and reduce stress. It also makes you feel better overall. Also, exercise helps people release built-up stress and energy, making them feel more balanced and focused.

Mindfulness meditation is when you focus on the here and now without judging. Practicing regularly can help decrease stress by making you feel more relaxed and aware of your feelings, and by helping you accept things as they are.

Deep breathing exercises like belly breathing can help your body relax and reduce stress. Breathe slowly and deeply for a few minutes every day to feel calm and relaxed.

Progressive Muscle Relaxation (PMR) means tightening and then releasing each muscle group in the body one by one. This method helps to relax the body and reduce stress, which makes it a good way to manage stress.

Regular exercise means doing physical activities like walking, running, swimming, or yoga on a regular basis. This can help to lower stress. Exercise makes the body release endorphins, which are natural mood boosters, and helps improve sleep. This is good for managing stress.

Eating healthy means eating a variety of fruits, veggies, whole grains, and lean proteins. This helps your body handle stress better. Don't have too much coffee, sugar, or processed foods because they can make you feel more stressed and anxious.

Make sure to get enough sleep every night because it is really important for managing stress and staying healthy. Develop a regular sleep schedule, have a calming bedtime routine, and make sure your bedroom is comfortable for sleeping.

Get close with people like your friends and family, or join groups that can help you. Talking to someone you trust about your stress can make you feel better and help you handle it better.

Managing your time well can help you feel less stressed. You can do this by deciding what is most important, setting achievable goals, and making sure you take breaks to relax and take care of yourself. Divide tasks into smaller parts and don't take on too much at once.

Reduce the amount of time you spend on screens and using media: Being constantly exposed to news, social media, and electronics can make you feel more stressed and overwhelmed. Set limits on how much time you spend on screens and make time for things that help you relax and connect with others in real life.

Try activities that involve both moving your body and using your mind, like yoga, tai chi, or qigong. These activities help you focus and relax at the same time. These activities can help lower stress, make you more flexible and strong, and keep you healthy overall.

Keeping a journal can help you deal with stress and understand your feelings. Writing about what you think and how you feel can make you feel better. Writing in a journal regularly can help you notice patterns, be thankful, and solve problems better.

Get help from a mental health expert if stress becomes too much for you to handle or gets in the way of your everyday life. Getting help from therapy, counseling, or support groups can give you useful ways to handle stress and make your mental health better.

Managing your time and deciding what to do first.

Focusing on what's most important: Being good at managing your time means figuring out what needs to be done first and making sure you have enough time and resources to do it. By organizing tasks by how important and urgent they are, people can concentrate on the most important things and reduce stress.

Making goals that are possible: making goals that you can actually reach helps people feel like they have control and feel proud of what they accomplish, even when things are tough. By breaking big goals into smaller tasks and celebrating little achievements along the way, people can stay motivated and less overwhelmed.

Creating healthy boundaries and taking care of yourself are important parts of managing stress well. Setting boundaries for how much we work and how many social commitments we have can help prevent feeling exhausted and overwhelmed. It's also important to prioritize taking care of ourselves by getting enough sleep, eating well, and taking time for leisure activities. This helps us to bounce back from challenges and stay healthy.

In summary, dealing with stress and anxiety is a complex task that involves knowing yourself, learning how to cope, and taking action to manage them. By finding out what makes you stressed and anxious, using strategies to manage stress, and being good at managing your time and taking care of yourself, you can become better at handling life's tough times.

Chapter 5: Encouraging Ways to Stay Healthy

In this chapter, we talk about how food, exercise, sleep, and other things we do every day can help us stay mentally healthy and feel good overall. By doing healthy things, people can make their bodies, minds, and brains work better. This can help prevent mental health problems and make life better.

Nutrition and exercise can affect how we feel mentally.

New research in nutritional psychiatry shows that what you eat can affect your mental health. Some foods like fish, nuts, and vegetables are good for your brain and mood. Eating a lot of processed foods and sugar can make you more likely to feel sad or worried.

Here are 10 herbs, fruits, and vegetables known for their benefits to digestion, immune system support, and fat burning:

Ginger: Known for its anti-inflammatory properties, ginger can aid digestion, reduce nausea, and support the immune system.

Turmeric: Contains curcumin, a powerful antioxidant with anti-inflammatory effects, which can aid digestion and boost the immune system.

Garlic: Supports immune function and has antimicrobial properties that can help with digestion. It also aids in fat metabolism.

Spinach: Rich in vitamins and minerals, including iron and fiber, spinach supports digestion and boosts the immune system.

Berries (such as blueberries, strawberries, and raspberries): Packed with antioxidants, vitamins, and fiber, berries support digestion, boost the immune system, and aid in fat burning.

Avocado: High in healthy fats and fiber, avocados support digestion, help regulate blood sugar levels, and promote fat burning.

Broccoli: Contains fiber and antioxidants that support digestion and boost the immune system. It also aids in fat metabolism.

Lemon: Rich in vitamin C and antioxidants, lemon can aid digestion, boost the immune system, and support fat burning.

Peppermint: Known for its soothing properties, peppermint can relieve digestive discomfort and support healthy digestion.

Green tea: Contains catechins, which have been shown to boost metabolism and aid in fat burning. Green tea also supports the immune system with its antioxidant properties.

Exercise and feeling good: Doing regular physical activity is good for your body and also helps you feel happy and healthy in your mind. Physical activity makes the body release feel-good chemicals called endorphins. This can help with depression, stress, and mood. Moreover, exercise helps the brain to change and adapt to new experiences, which can make thinking and memory better.

Good sleep habits and why they are important for mental health.

Sleep is really important for our mental health and thinking abilities. Good sleep helps us think better and be healthier. When you sleep, your brain carries out important tasks like organizing memories, controlling emotions, and repairing itself. These things are necessary to keep your mind healthy. Not getting enough sleep for a long time can lead to problems like feeling moody, having trouble thinking clearly, and other mental health issues.

How to Sleep Better: To sleep well, do things that help you relax and rest. This means keeping a regular sleep schedule, doing calming things before bed, making sure your sleep environment is comfortable, and avoiding screens and exciting activities before you go to sleep.

Preventing Drug Misuse and Its Impact on Mental Health.

Using drugs or alcohol can really harm how you feel and think. Using drugs or other substances may help you feel better for a little while, but in the long run, they can make anxiety, depression, and other mental health problems worse. Furthermore, using drugs or alcohol can make it hard to think clearly, cause problems with relationships, and make it difficult to do daily activities. This can worsen mental health problems. Ways to Help: People who have problems with drugs can use harm-reduction strategies to stay safer and make healthier choices. This could mean not using as much drugs or alcohol, talking to doctors or groups for help, and trying other ways to deal with problems like therapy, meditation, or being active.

In summary, it's important to encourage healthy habits to help with mental health and feeling good overall. By eating healthy, exercising, getting enough sleep, and not using drugs, people can improve their bodies and minds, lower the chances of mental health problems, and make their lives better.

Chapter 6: Getting Help from Experts

In this chapter, we talk about how it's important to know when you need to get help for your mental health. We'll also learn about the different kinds of mental health professionals you can talk to, and ways to deal with the stigma that comes with getting therapy.

Knowing When to Ask for Professional Help.

It's important to know when to get professional help for mental health issues so you can get the right help at the right time. In this article, we talk about why it's important to notice the signs of mental health problems and give advice on when to think about getting help from a mental health doctor.

Understanding how people feel and behave when they have mental health problems.

Mental health problems can look very different for each person. They can affect how you feel, think, and act in many different ways. Some common signs of mental health problems can include always feeling sad, worried, or afraid, having big mood changes, being easily annoyed, having trouble focusing, changes in eating or sleeping and thinking about hurting yourself or ending your life.

It's important to notice if your thoughts, feelings, or actions are changing and affecting your daily life for a long time. Sometimes feeling moody or stressed is okay, but if you feel this way a lot or very strongly, it could be a sign of a mental health problem. You should talk to a professional for help.

Effects on everyday activities

One important sign to look for when you should ask a professional for help is how much mental health symptoms are getting in the way of your daily life. If your symptoms make it hard for you to do important things like work, school, or taking care of yourself, it could mean you have a serious mental health problem.

If someone feels really sad or worried a lot and that stops them from going to work or school, being with others, or doing things they used to like, they may need to get professional help. Likewise, if someone starts acting differently, like using more drugs, staying away from people, or doing dangerous things, they may need to see a professional for help.

Length of time and how long symptoms last.

Another thing to think about is how long mental health symptoms last and how often they happen. It's okay to feel different moods or stressed sometimes, but if these feelings last a long time or make it hard to do everyday things, it might mean there's a bigger problem.

For instance, if you feel sad, worried, or cranky for a long time, even though you try to take care of yourself, it might mean you need to see a doctor. In the same way, if symptoms get worse over time or start to affect many parts of your life, it's important to get help from a mental health expert.

In the end, knowing when to get professional help for mental health problems means paying attention to the signs and symptoms of mental illness, thinking about how they affect your daily life, and how long they last. Individuals can get the help they need to deal with mental health problems and improve their overall well-being by seeking evaluation and treatment early.

Different kinds of mental health experts and what they do.

- Doctors who specialize in mental health disorders are called psychiatrists. They diagnose and treat people with mental health problems. They have permission to give medicine and can also give therapy or other kinds of treatment.

- Psychologists are highly qualified therapists who have studied psychology at a university and are trained to understand, diagnose, and help people with mental health problems using talk therapy and other treatments. They can't give medication, but they can work with psychiatrists or other healthcare providers as part of a team to treat patients.

Licensed Clinical Social Workers (LCSWs) are people who have been trained to help with mental health problems. They talk to and support individuals, families, and groups. They can focus on different areas like helping people with drugs, dealing with difficult experiences, or working with families. They usually work in hospitals or have their own office.

- Licensed Professional Counselors (LPCs) are trained to help people with mental health, relationships, and life changes. They can work in their own office, local mental health centers, or other places where people get treatment.

Breaking the shame around getting therapy.

Changing people's wrong ideas: Many people think badly about mental health and getting therapy, which can stop people from getting help when they really need it. By changing wrong ideas and beliefs about mental illness and therapy, we can make an environment that is more supportive and includes everyone and also encourages people to seek help when they need it.

Getting therapy is a good way to take care of yourself and grow, instead of showing weakness or failure. By making therapy seem normal and useful for dealing with mental health issues, we can make it less shameful to ask for help from a professional.

Talking openly and honestly about mental health and therapy can help remove misunderstandings and wrong ideas about them. This can make it easier for people to get help. We can create a welcoming and understanding environment for mental health issues by talking about our own experiences, helping, and giving the right information to others.

In summary, asking for help from a professional for mental health issues is a brave and positive step towards getting better and improving yourself. By learning about the signs of mental health problems, understanding the job of mental health experts, and not being ashamed to get help, people can find the support they need to do well.

Chapter 7: 20 Ways to Improve Mental Health

1. ***Be thankful for what you have and think good thoughts about yourself.***

Make a habit of being thankful every day: Spend some time each day thinking about the things you appreciate. This could be things like enjoying a hot cup of coffee in the morning, seeing someone you care about smile, or being out in nature. Writing in a gratitude journal every day can help you think about the good things in life and feel more positive. It's a powerful way to focus on what you're thankful for.

Show you are thankful: Don't be afraid to thank others. Expressing gratitude can help strengthen relationships and make people feel connected and positive. It could be thanking a friend, recognizing a coworker's effort, or complimenting a stranger's kindness.

Use positive statements to remind yourself that you are valuable, capable, and have potential. Using positive phrases every day can help change negative thoughts and make you feel more confident and hopeful. You can say them out loud, write them down, or imagine them in your mind. Positive affirmations are statements that we tell ourselves to feel good about ourselves. For example, "I am worthy of love and respect," "I can overcome challenges," and "I deserve to be happy and fulfilled. "

Pay attention to what's happening right now: Practicing mindfulness can help you enjoy the present moment and find happiness in everyday things. Instead of thinking about the things you regret from the past or feeling anxious about what might happen in the future, just concentrate on what is happening right now. Pause and enjoy the things you see, hear, and feel around you. It could be the sun on your skin, the birds singing, or your favorite food.

Start and finish your day in a positive way: Do something positive in the morning and before bed to make you feel happy and thankful. Start your day with a few minutes of quiet thinking or end your day by thinking about three things you are thankful for. Doing these things regularly can help you feel more positive and thankful in your life.

By being thankful and using positive thoughts every day, you can become more hopeful, handle problems better, and feel happier and more satisfied.

1. *Participate in regular physical activity.*

Try to do exercise regularly because it's important for your mental health. Try to exercise regularly, whether it's every day, a few times a week, or whenever it works best for you. Regular exercise helps control emotions, lower stress, and improve overall health.

Do things you like: Exercise doesn't have to be hard or at the gym. The important thing is to find things you really like to do and are excited about. Pick activities that make you happy and fulfilled, like dancing or playing sports, so you can keep up with your exercise routine for a long time.

Trying different things is important for staying interested and keeping up with your exercise. Mix up your workouts with cardio, weights, and stretching to keep it fun and push your body in new ways. Trying new things can make your workouts more interesting and fun.

Make realistic goals: Decide on achievable goals for your exercise routine, like getting stronger or feeling healthier. Divide big goals into smaller, easy steps, and be happy about the progress you make. Setting goals gives you something to work towards and helps you stay motivated and accountable.

Think about how exercising makes you feel, not just how you look or wanting to be fit. This can be a stronger reason to keep exercising. Make sure to think about all the good things that come from being active, like having more energy, feeling happier, sleeping better, and just enjoying life more.

Exercise with friends or family to make it more fun. Try working out with your friends or joining group exercise classes or sports teams. It's a great way to make exercise more fun and social. Exercising with people can make workouts more fun, give you social support, and help you stay committed to your goals.

Pay attention to what your body is telling you and change your exercise routine if needed. It's okay to feel tired and sore when you exercise, but if you push too much or don't listen to your body, you could get hurt or feel too exhausted. Take care of yourself by making rest, recovery, and good food a priority to help your body and mind stay healthy.

Exercising regularly and taking care of your body can make you feel happier, less stressed, more confident, and overall healthier. Make sure to do the activities you like the most and set goals that you can actually achieve. Pay attention to how your body feels and make sure to keep exercising in a way that is good for both your mind and body in the long run.

1. *Focus on taking care of yourself.*

Know why taking care of yourself is important: Taking care of yourself is not being selfish. It's important for staying healthy and strong. Taking time for self-care activities helps you to relax, feel better, and take care of your body and mind. Understand that looking after yourself isn't just good for you, but it also helps you to be your best in other parts of your life.

Figure out what makes you feel good: Self-care is different for everyone, so it's important to find activities and practices that make you happy. Think about the things that make you happy, calm, and satisfied, like reading, taking a bath, doing yoga, or being in nature. Listen to your body and feelings to figure out what things you need to do for self-care.

Take time to take care of yourself: In today's busy world, we usually focus on other things instead of taking care of ourselves. But, taking care of yourself means making time in your schedule for things that make you feel good mentally, physically, and spiritually. Make sure to take care of yourself regularly by scheduling breaks during the day and setting aside time every week for self-care. It's important to make self-care a regular part of your routine.

Be nice to yourself and treat yourself with the same kindness and understanding you would give to a friend. Recognize what you can't do, accept that nobody is perfect, and stop being hard on yourself. Self-care is not about being perfect, but about being kind to yourself, especially when things are tough.

Set limits: Creating limits is an important part of taking care of yourself, because it helps you protect your time, energy, and health. Learn how to refuse to do things, or commit to things, or be in relationships that make you feel tired or don't match with what's important to you. Creating limits helps you to take care of yourself and respect your needs without feeling bad or angry.

Take care of yourself by being present and mindful when doing self-care activities. It will make them more effective and enjoyable.

Enjoying a tasty meal, taking a relaxing bath, or going for a walk in nature helps you be grateful and feel happy in the present moment.

Ask for help when you need it: If you need help, don't be afraid to ask friends, family, or mental health experts. Creating a group of people you trust who understand and respect your need to take care of yourself can help you feel supported, validated, and accountable as you take care of yourself.

Taking care of yourself is important for staying healthy and balanced in life. By taking care of yourself, making time for self-care, being kind to yourself, setting limits, and doing activities that relax you, you can make your life healthier, happier, and more satisfying.

1. *Connect with the natural world.*

Spend time outside: In today's busy world with lots of technology, it's easy to stop spending time in nature. Make an effort to spend time outside in nature as much as you can to feel connected to the natural world. Spending time in nature, like going for a walk in the mountains or a park, or just sitting in your backyard, can make you feel better emotionally and mentally.

Feel better by spending time in nature: Being in nature can make you feel calmer, less stressed, and more relaxed. The things we see, hear, and feel in nature can make us feel amazed, curious, and calm. This can help reduce feelings of being worried, sad, and stressed. Take a moment to look at the beautiful and detailed things in nature, like the pretty colors of a sunset or the sound of leaves blowing in the wind.

Spend time in nature and focus on being present and mindful. Use all your senses to pay attention to what you see, hear, smell, and feel around you. Breathe in the fresh air, feel the sun on your skin, and listen to the birds or water. By focusing on the present, you can feel more connected and calm.

Enjoy being outside: Doing activities outside can make you healthier. It can give you a stronger heart, more vitamin D, and a better immune system. Doing exercise outside, like running or biking, can make you feel happier and give you more energy.

Take care of the Earth: Being close to nature helps you understand and value the environment. Think about how you interact with the Earth and find ways to reduce your impact on the environment and support sustainability every day. Doing things like using less, saving energy, and helping out with eco-friendly projects all help to save the Earth for the next generations.

Add nature to your everyday life: Try to bring nature into your daily routine, even if you live in a busy city. Adding nature to your daily life, like going for a walk in the park or keeping plants at home, can make you feel calm and connected.

Invite friends, family, or loved ones to join you in outdoor activities: Spend time outside with friends and family by going on a picnic, camping, or walking in nature. It will make your relationships stronger and you'll have special memories to cherish.

Get outside, be mindful, and do outdoor activities to feel peaceful, refreshed, and connected to nature. Spend time connecting with nature and you will feel better in your mind, heart, and body. Nature has many benefits for your health.

1. **Find something you enjoy doing in your free time, like a hobby or a creative activity.**

Find something you enjoy doing in your free time, like a hobby or a creative activity.

Find what you love: Spend some time trying out different hobbies and creative activities to see what makes you feel happy and satisfied. Try different things like painting, writing, cooking, gardening, playing music, or learning new skills to find out what you like and are good at.

Find time to be creative: In our busy lives, it's easy to forget about doing creative things because we have so many important things to do. However, it's important to make time for being creative because it helps your mind and emotions stay healthy. Make sure to set aside time every week to do the hobby or creative activity that you love. Think of it as an important way to take care of yourself and grow as a person.

Embrace the Process: Pay attention to how you make things, not just what you make in the end. Give yourself the chance to really get into the creative process and have fun trying new things and expressing yourself. Stop trying to be perfect and judging yourself, instead, be curious, playful, and open to new ideas.

Express yourself by being creative: Being creative allows you to communicate and express yourself. Express your feelings and ideas through art, writing, or music. Be creative in solving problems or coming up with new ideas. Let yourself be free to express yourself without holding back.

Doing creative things can make you really focused and in the moment. You might not even notice the time passing. This feeling of flow feels really good and refreshing. It helps you escape from the daily worries and stresses. Give in to the creative process and feel happy and satisfied. Connect with others and build a community by sharing your creative activities. This can help you feel more connected and a sense of belonging. Find chances to meet people who have the same interests as you. You can do this by joining art or writing groups or going to creative workshops and events. Creating a group of creative people can help you stay motivated, get ideas, and feel supported as you work on your projects.

Celebrate how creative you are and the special things you can do. Understand how important it is to be creative, whether it's for fun, figuring out more about yourself, or helping others. Be happy and proud of the things you create, even if they're not perfect, and let yourself feel happy and fulfilled by being creative.

By doing something you enjoy, like a hobby or being creative, you can use your natural creativity and feel happy expressing yourself. This can help with your mental and emotional health. If you like painting, writing, cooking, gardening, or doing anything creative, take the time to do it and let your creativity shine.

1. Practice taking deep breaths and try to relax your body.

Breathing deeply can help reduce stress and make you feel relaxed. It's a simple and strong technique that can help. By taking slow, deep breaths using your diaphragm, you can make your body relax and reduce the physical effects of stress and anxiety. Make sure to do deep breathing exercises often. Breathe in slowly through your nose and let your belly rise. Then exhale slowly through your mouth. Make sure to take deep breaths every day, especially when you're feeling stressed before you go to bed, or when you are practicing mindfulness or meditation.

Progressive Muscle Relaxation is a way to relax your body and mind by tightening and relaxing different muscle groups. First, squeeze a body part like your shoulders or fists for a few seconds. Then, let go and let the muscles relax. Relax your entire body by moving through each muscle group from your head to your toes, gradually releasing tension. Regularly do progressive muscle relaxation, especially when you feel stressed or tense, to release muscle tension, decrease anxiety, and improve your overall well-being.

Guided imagery and visualization are methods to relax by using your imagination to create peaceful images in your mind. Picture yourself in a calm and relaxing place like a beach, forest, or mountaintop. Close your eyes and think about it. Use your imagination to see, hear, smell, and feel everything in your made-up world. Really get into the experience. Use thinking about peaceful scenes to feel calm inside and reduce stress and anxiety. This can help you relax and feel good.

Mindfulness meditation is when you focus on the present moment with an open and curious mind. Sit still and pay attention to your breathing, how your body feels, or the sounds around you. Let your thoughts and feelings come and go without judging them or holding onto them. Practice being aware and focused by paying attention to what you're doing and feeling, and being kind to yourself. Whenever your mind starts to wander, gently bring it back to what's happening right now. Try doing mindfulness meditation often to lower stress, be more aware of yourself, and feel more peaceful and balanced in your life.

Yoga and Tai Chi are activities that help the body and mind. They include stretching, breathing exercises, and meditation to help you relax, be more flexible, and think clearly. Practice yoga or tai chi regularly to feel less stressed, get fitter, and feel better overall. Concentrate on moving slowly and carefully while breathing deeply and rhythmically. This helps you to be aware of your body and breath in the moment. Add yoga or tai chi to your weekly schedule to feel relaxed and balanced in both your body and mind.

Make a relaxation plan: Make a routine that includes different ways to relax that you like and that help you feel better. Try different ways of relaxing, like taking deep breaths, tensing and relaxing your muscles, imagining calm places, staying focused on the present, doing yoga, or practicing tai chi, to see which one helps you the most. Make time each day to do relaxation exercises. You can do them in the morning, during breaks, or in the evening. It will help you calm down, recharge, and get ready for sleep. Being consistent with relaxation techniques is important. Make relaxation a priority every day to feel better and have more peace of mind.

1. Set goals that you can actually achieve and then celebrate when you reach them.

Start by choosing clear and realistic goals that match what you value, like, and want to achieve. Think about what you want to achieve in your life, like getting better at something, getting ahead in your job, being healthy, or building better relationships. It's important to understand why these things are important to you. Break big goals into smaller, doable steps to make them easier to achieve and act on.

Create clear and achievable goals using SMART criteria. Make sure they are measurable, relevant, and have a time limit. By creating specific, achievable, and realistic goals, you give yourself a plan for success and improve your chances of getting things done.

For instance, instead of saying you want to "get in shape," you could make a specific goal like "run a 5K race in six months by jogging three times a week. "

Make a plan: After you decide what you want to achieve, make a plan with all the steps you need to follow to reach your goals. Divide each goal into smaller tasks or goals, set deadlines for them, and prioritize them based on how important and urgent they are. Having a clear plan helps you stay focused, organized, and motivated as you work towards your goals.

Keep an eye on how you're doing: Check regularly to see if you are moving forward and getting closer to your goals. Remember what you have achieved, the challenges you have faced, and the things you have learned. Change your plans if necessary to overcome obstacles and stay focused on your goals. Keeping an eye on how you're doing helps you see how you're doing and can help keep you motivated and committed to reaching your goals.

Celebrate what you've done: It's important to celebrate the things you've achieved, even if they seem small, to recognize the effort and commitment you've put in. Make sure you give yourself credit and celebrate when you achieve something important, like going out for something fun, eating your favorite food, or taking a moment to think about what you've accomplished. Celebrating what you accomplish makes you feel good and gives you the energy to keep working towards your goals.

Learn from when things are hard and when you don't do things perfectly: See them as chances to get better and learn. Instead of seeing failure as losing, think of it as a lesson that can help you do better next time. Think about what didn't work, find ways to do better, and change the way you do things. When things go wrong, think of them as temporary problems that you can overcome. Stay positive and keep working towards your goals.

Stay open to changes and be willing to adapt to achieve your goals, knowing that things may change and you may need to make changes as you go. Be ready for new chances, different ways of doing things, and unexpected changes that may help you reach your goals. By being able to move quickly and adapt to changes, you can deal with problems better and keep moving forward towards your goals.

It's important to set achievable goals and celebrate when you reach them. This will help you stay motivated, and focused, and feel a sense of success in your life. By setting goals, making a plan, keeping track of how you're doing, and celebrating when you do well, you can have a positive and active way of reaching your goals and making your dreams come true.

1. **Avoiding too much bad news and using social media less often.**

Understand how watching news and using social media can affect your feelings and mental health. Hearing too much bad news and seeing scary headlines and negative posts on social media can make you feel more anxious, scared, and sad. This can lead to feeling stressed and overwhelmed. Pay attention to what you watch or read because it can affect how you feel and think.

Decide how much time you will spend on media to keep your mind and emotions healthy. Spend less time watching the news, using social media, or getting into online discussions that make you feel bad. Choose certain times of the day to use media, like morning or evening, so you can stay updated without feeling too stressed or upset.

Choose carefully where you get your news and information from. Find trustworthy sources that give correct and fair news, instead of exaggerated or one-sided information. You can stop following or mute accounts on social media that regularly share sad or upsetting things, and instead, follow accounts that make you feel good or teach you something.

Be aware of how media affects you. Pay attention to what you watch, read, and hear. Think about how it makes you feel. Take breaks from using social media or watching TV when it makes you feel bad. Take time to relax by doing things like being outside, doing meditation, or spending time with family and friends in person.

Try to find sources of positive news and uplifting content that make you feel hopeful, strong, and caring. Find stories about people being nice, giving to others, and making things better in your area and other places. Continuously look for things that inspire and make you feel good, to help balance out all the negative stuff you might see on TV or online.

Do things that make you happy and give you a sense of purpose. Spend time on things and people that make you happy and feel good. Do things that make you happy, like doing art, helping others, or spending time with family and friends. Focus on things that make you feel good and bring positivity to your life.

Make self-care a part of your everyday routine to support your mental and emotional health. Take part in things that help you relax, reduce stress, and keep your emotions in balance. This can include things like exercising, meditating, writing in a journal, or doing something creative. Make sure to take care of yourself to protect against the bad effects of media and to build up your strength to deal with tough times. To keep your mind healthy, try to avoid bad news and too much time on social media. Instead, focus on good things and things that make you feel good. This can help you stay positive and feel better about life. Don't forget that you can choose what you read and watch, and how it makes you feel. Choose to focus on positive and empowering sources of information and content.

1. Volunteer or be kind to others.

Experience the happiness of helping others: Volunteering or doing kind things for others is not only good for the people receiving help, but it also feels really good for the person giving it. Volunteering lets you help causes you care about, make a good difference in your community, and meet others who care about the same things you do. Volunteering is when you help others without getting paid. You can do things like serving food to people in need, cleaning up the environment, or working for a charity. It's a chance to make a positive impact on other people's lives and feel good about what you're doing.
Find what matters to you: Think about what you like, what you are good at, and what you believe in when deciding how to help others. Think about what is important to you, like helping schools, standing up for fairness, or taking care of animals. Look for chances to help out that match what you care about and what you are good at. This will let you make a real and sincere difference to the causes that matter to you.
Make time to help others: Choose to spend some of your time volunteering or doing kind things for others. Schedule time to do

things that help people in a meaningful way. Make sure to give back to others regularly. This could mean volunteering a few hours each week or doing little acts of kindness every day. Make time to help others with your family, friends, or a group, working together to make a big difference.

Feel the good effects of being kind to others: Doing volunteer work or being kind can help your mind, feelings, and body feel better. Studies have found that being nice to others can make you happier, less stressed, and healthier. Volunteering can help you learn new things, connect with others, and feel good about yourself. It can also help you develop skills and grow as a person.

Be nice every day by doing small acts of kindness, not just at organized volunteer events. Little acts of kindness, like smiling at a stranger, helping a neighbor, or thanking someone who helped you, can spread happiness and goodwill. By being kind and compassionate to others, you help make the world a more caring and connected place.

Celebrate how you are helping others by volunteering and being kind, no matter how small your actions may seem. Celebrate the difference you're making in people's lives, in communities, and for important issues. Remember that every little thing you do makes a difference. Tell others about what you've done and what you're proud of. Encourage them to help out and make good changes in the world with you.

Encourage others to join in: Show your love for helping out and being kind to motivate others to join in and make a positive impact. Tell your friends, family, and coworkers about what you did, why you did it, and how it made a difference. Encourage them to also do something helpful in their own way. You can inspire others to be kind and helpful by showing them how to do it and talking about kindness and helping others. This can help make the world a more caring place.

Volunteering and being kind doesn't just help others, it also makes you feel happy and gives meaning to your life. Help out in any way you can, like volunteering, being kind every day, or encouraging others to join in. It's important to give back and make a good difference in your community and the world.

1. Try being mindful and meditating to keep your mind healthy.

Practicing mindfulness and meditation has many advantages for your mental, emotional, and physical health. These practices include being aware of the present moment, watching thoughts and feelings without judgment, and concentrating on the breath or other focal points. Here's why it's important to practice mindfulness and meditation every day and the good things it can do for you.

Decrease Stress and Worry: Mindfulness and meditation can help you feel more relaxed and calm, which can lower stress and anxiety. By paying attention to what's happening right now and not worrying about what happened before or what might happen later, you can feel less stressed and not so worried. Practicing regularly helps the mind get better at dealing with stress, making you more able to handle tough situations and stay emotionally steady.

Get better at focusing and thinking clearly: Mindfulness and meditation help you focus and think better by training your brain to pay attention and not get distracted. By paying attention to the present moment, you can teach your mind to concentrate on what you're doing right now, like studying, working, or being creative. Better focus and thinking clearly help you get more done and do it better in your daily tasks.

Improve controlling your emotions: Being mindful and meditating help you become more aware of your thoughts, emotions, and how your body feels. By paying attention to how you feel inside without getting upset or making quick judgments, you can become stronger emotionally and feel more balanced. Mindfulness helps you to be kind to yourself when you feel emotions and not just react quickly or feel overwhelmed by bad feelings.

Practice being kind to yourself and accepting who you are: Mindfulness and meditation help you be less critical of yourself and your life experiences. By paying attention to your thoughts and feelings in a curious and kind way, you can become more aware of yourself and be nicer to yourself. This helps you to accept and be okay with your strengths and weaknesses, which makes you feel better about yourself and able to handle tough times.

Encourage Physical Relaxation and Health: Meditation and mindfulness help the body relax and reduce stress, by lowering heart rate, blood pressure, and cortisol levels. Practicing regularly can help your muscles feel less tense, make you sleep better, and make your immune system stronger, which can make your body feel better and more energetic.

Improve Relationships and Communication: Being more mindful and meditating helps people to understand others better, be kinder, and become better listeners, which makes their relationships and communication better. By practicing being aware of the present moment and listening without reacting, you can become better at understanding and connecting with others. "Mindfulness can also make it easier for you to handle conflicts and tough situations with more emotional smarts and ability. "

Help people grow spiritually and feel connected: For lots of folks, being mindful and meditating helps them feel more peaceful and connected to others, and helps them understand their purpose in life. By focusing on the present and feeling connected to something bigger than yourself, you can feel really amazed, thankful, and spiritual. Practicing mindfulness can help us think about life's big questions, find purpose, and feel more spiritually fulfilled.

Help with Feeling Sad and Stressed: Mindfulness activities can help make you feel better if you are sad, stressed, or have other mood problems like PTSD. By practicing being more aware of the present moment and not reacting to difficult emotions, people can learn to deal with their thoughts and feelings in a better and kinder way. This can help to make depressive symptoms go down and improve overall mental health.

Get better sleep and beat insomnia: Being mindful and meditating can make your sleep better and help you sleep peacefully by making you feel relaxed, reducing anxiety, and calming your mind. By doing mindfulness exercises like relaxing your muscles or meditating before bed, you can get ready for a good sleep. Mindfulness techniques can help people sleep better and have better attitudes about sleep, which can make their sleep better in the long run.

Improve Life: Mindfulness and meditation help people become more aware of themselves, stay strong, and feel better, leading to a better quality of life. By focusing on the present and being kind to yourself, you can handle life's challenges better. Practicing mindfulness can help you feel more happy and satisfied in your daily life.

Adding mindfulness and meditation to your daily schedule can help improve your mental, emotional, and physical health in a big way. Whether you do meditation or just pay attention to what you're doing, like eating or walking, you can feel more peaceful, think more clearly, and be stronger in everything you do. Start with little steps and keep practicing mindfulness and meditation. Enjoy how it helps your health and happiness.

1. Eat healthy food and drink enough water.

Eating healthy food and drinking enough water is really important for your overall health. They can make a big difference in how you feel physically, mentally, and emotionally. Here's why these practices are important:

Eat healthy foods that are full of nutrients to keep your body healthy and strong. Eating a variety of nutrient-rich foods is very important for staying physically and mentally healthy. Try to eat different types of fruits, vegetables, whole grains, lean meats, and healthy fats in your meals. These foods have important nutrients that help keep our bodies healthy and strong, protect our brains, and keep us feeling good.

Make sure you drink enough water: It's really important to stay hydrated to keep your body working well and to stay healthy. Water is very important for our body. It helps to keep our body at the right temperature, get rid of bad substances, make our joints work smoothly, and help us digest food. Try to drink at least 8 glasses of water every day. You might need to drink more if you are active or if the weather is hot. Everyone's water needs are different, so pay attention to how much water you need.

Choose natural foods over processed foods: Go for foods that are whole and minimally processed whenever you can. These foods have more nutrients and less added sugars, bad fats, and artificial chemicals. Eat less processed and ultra-processed foods, like sugary snacks, fast food, and convenience meals, because they can cause inflammation, make you gain weight, and lead to long-term health problems if you have too much.

Eat mindfully: Pay attention to when you are hungry or full, and focus on the taste and feel of the food. Eat slowly and enjoy each bite, think about how the food tastes, feels, and smells. Don't use screens or do too many things at once while you eat. It can make you eat too much without thinking and give you bad digestion. Pay attention to your body's cues for being hungry and full, and stop eating when you feel content, not overly full.

Eat different kinds of healthy foods: Add lots of different colorful fruits and vegetables to your meals so you can get lots of vitamins, minerals, and antioxidants. Try cooking in different ways and trying new flavors and styles of food to make your meals more fun and tasty. Use lean protein sources like chicken, fish, tofu, beans, and lentils, and also eat healthy fats from nuts, seeds, avocado, and olive oil.

Plan and make meals and snacks ahead of time so you don't have to eat unhealthy fast food or convenience food. Cook a lot of food at once, divide it into portions, and put it in containers so you can easily take it with you on busy days. Fill your kitchen with healthy foods and ingredients, and try different ways of preparing meals that fit into your schedule and the foods you like.

Be careful about eating too many sugary snacks, desserts, and drinks, as well as processed foods with lots of sugar, bad fats, and salt. It's fine to have these foods sometimes as part of a balanced diet, but try to eat them less and focus more on whole, healthy foods as the main part of your diet. When you want a snack, pick healthy options like fruit, yogurt, nuts, or homemade snacks.

Remember to drink water throughout the day by keeping a refillable water bottle with you and taking small sips frequently. Start your day by drinking a glass of water, and try to drink water before, during, and after meals, and also during and after you exercise. Make sure to look for signs that you are not drinking enough water, like having a dry mouth, dark pee, feeling tired, or having headaches. If you see these signs, drink more water.

Pay attention to what your body is telling you. Eat when you're hungry, drink when you're thirsty, and stop eating when you're full. Eat when you are hungry and stop when you feel full, instead of following strict rules about when to eat. Respect when your body tells you it's hungry or full, and believe that it can take care of itself to stay healthy and energized.

Get help from a professional if you need it: If you don't know how to make a healthy diet, or if you have special diet needs or health problems, talk to a registered dietitian or nutritionist for advice. These experts can give you personalized advice, and meal schedules, and help to reach your health and wellness goals.

By eating well and drinking water, you can keep your body healthy, support your mental and emotional health, and have lots of energy. Make small changes to your eating and drinking habits that you can keep doing. Be happy about how they make you healthier and improve your life. Always eat well and drink plenty of water to stay healthy for a long time.

1. Get enough good sleep for your health.

Getting enough good sleep is really important for keeping your body and mind healthy. Getting good sleep is very important for your body. It helps with things like remembering things, thinking clearly, staying healthy, and feeling happy. Here's why it's important to get enough good sleep:

It is really important to get enough good sleep because it makes our body healthy and helps us feel good. When you sleep, your body does important things like fixing tissues, controlling hormones, and making memories stronger. Getting enough sleep helps you feel happier, think better, stay healthy, and manage stress. Understanding how important sleep is can make you want to focus on getting enough rest and change the way you sleep if needed.

Create a regular sleep routine by going to bed and waking up at the same time every day, even on weekends. Consistency helps to keep your body's internal clock on track, which helps you sleep better and feel better overall. Try to get seven to nine hours of sleep each night, based on what feels best for you.

Make a Calm Bedtime Plan: Make a calming bedtime plan to tell your body it's time to relax and get ready for sleep. Do relaxing things like reading, taking a warm bath, doing relaxation exercises, or listening to calming music before going to bed. Don't do things that make you excited or use electronic devices like phones and computers before bed, as they can stop you from sleeping.

Improve Your Sleep Place: Make your bedroom a place that helps you relax and feel comfortable when you want to sleep. Make sure your bedroom is dark, quiet, and not too warm. Buy a comfy mattress, pillows, and bedding. Reduce loud sounds and disturbances, like phones or animals, and think about using curtains that block out light or machines that make soothing sounds to keep away things that bother you. Make your bedroom a peaceful place for sleeping, to help you rest and sleep without any interruptions.

Avoid drinking coffee or smoking before bed: They can make it harder for you to sleep. Also, don't drink too much alcohol because it can make it hard for you to sleep well. Instead, choose calming herbal teas or warm milk, which can help you relax and fall asleep easier.

Try using relaxation techniques: Do them before bed to help you relax and reduce stress before you go to sleep. You can try breathing deeply, relaxing your muscles, imagining calming scenes, or meditating to relax your mind and body before going to sleep. Try different methods to see what helps you sleep better at night, and then make them part of your bedtime routine.

Keep track of your sleep: Keep an eye on how you sleep and how well you sleep, and change things if you need to so you can sleep better. Write down when you go to sleep and when you wake up every day. Also write down things that might make it hard for you to sleep, like feeling stressed, drinking coffee, or things in your environment. Use apps or gadgets that track your sleep to see how long and how well you sleep. Look for any trends in your sleep that show where you can make it better.

Get help if you have trouble sleeping: If you can't sleep well even after trying everything, ask a doctor for help. Speak to your doctor or a sleep expert about your sleep problems, and consider treatments like therapy or medicine if needed. Improving problems with sleeping can help make your sleep better and also help your mental health.

Getting good sleep is really important for keeping your body and mind healthy and happy. You can sleep better by developing good sleep habits, making your sleep environment comfortable, and asking for help when you need it. This will help you feel more rested and get all the benefits of a good night's sleep. Make sure to prioritize sleep in taking care of yourself, and you will feel more refreshed, energetic, and strong every day.

1. Spend time with your friends and family often.

Spending time with friends and family and joining in social activities is important for keeping a healthy mind and body. People need friends and relationships to be happy and feel like they belong. Connecting with others helps us feel strong and able to handle our feelings. Here are a few ways to do more of this practice:

Spend lots of time with your loved ones: Make it a priority to spend time with them in your life. Plan to meet up regularly with your family, friends, or special person to do fun things together. Spend time with your family, friends, and partner regularly to make good memories and strengthen your relationships.

Have deeper talks with loved ones to make stronger connections: Don't just talk about little things, have more meaningful conversations. Listen carefully when others talk, show that you care about what they think and feel, and share openly about your own experiences and feelings. Ask interesting questions, tell stories, and create a space where people feel comfortable and connected.

Celebrate when your loved ones reach goals or do something important. Acknowledge and be happy for them when they have special moments in their lives. If someone has achieved something, like a birthday or a graduation, be sure to acknowledge and celebrate their success. Organize special parties or do nice things to show your support and feel happy about their achievements.

Be there for your loved ones during good and tough times to give them support and encouragement. Listen carefully to their worries, understand how they feel, and say supportive and reassuring words to them. Be there and ready to give support with a shoulder to lean on, an ear to listen, or a comforting hug when someone needs it. Your help can make a big difference in how they feel and how well they can handle things.

Spend time doing things you enjoy with your family and friends to make your relationships stronger. Spend time doing things you both like, like cooking, hiking, playing sports, or going to concerts, to have fun together on a regular basis. When you do things together, you make special memories and feel closer to each other.

Show thanks and appreciation to the people who are important to you: Take a moment to tell them how much you appreciate them. Express your love, appreciation, and thanks by speaking, showing through actions, or writing a note. Tell your family and friends how much you appreciate and love them. Developing a thankful mindset makes your relationships stronger and helps everyone feel appreciated and valued.

Keep in touch with family and friends who live far away by using technology and communication tools. Plan to have regular phone calls, video chats, or virtual meetups to stay in touch and hear about what's going on in each other's lives. Share pictures, videos, and news to stay connected and involved in each other's daily lives and important moments. Distance can keep you far away, but technology can help you stay connected and close.

Deal with problems and disagreements: Talk openly and kindly about any issues or misunderstandings in your relationships, and treat others with respect. Listen carefully, talk honestly, and work as a team to find solutions that everyone is happy with. Be ready to say sorry, forgive, and forget any bad feelings that might be stopping your relationship from being strong. Solving problems together in a healthy way makes relationships stronger and helps people trust and understand each other more.

Create special activities and customs: Make special things that you do together with your family or friends to help bring you closer. Gather with your loved ones regularly for activities and traditions that bring you closer together and make you feel like you belong. This will help you build strong connections and keep feeling connected. Rituals and traditions help us feel stable, know what to expect, and stay connected in a world that is always changing.

Help your family and friends when they go through big life changes, like getting married, having a baby, changing jobs, or losing someone. Help them with everyday things, be there for them when they need to talk, and support them through good and bad times in life. Celebrate when they do well and be there for them when things are hard. Your being here and helping means a lot during times when things are changing.

By spending time with friends and family and keeping in touch with them, you can build a strong support system, feel like you belong, and be happier in your life. Spend time with people who are important to you, show them you care, and treasure the relationships that make your life better. Your relationships with others are really important and can give you strength, the ability to bounce back from difficult times, and happiness. So, put a lot of effort into your relationships and you will benefit from having strong and fulfilling connections with others.

1. Get help from a group of people or a community online.

Getting help from a support group or online community can help improve your mental health and make you feel better. These communities help people with similar problems feel safe and supported. They can share their stories, cheer each other on, and give useful advice and resources. Here's how you can get more help from a support group or online community:

Look for a group or community online that can help you: Find one that is focused on the things you need and like. If you are dealing with mental health problems, long-term illness, overcoming addiction, grief, parenting difficulties, or other challenges in life, there are many groups and communities you can join online or in person. Find groups that you connect with and that help you achieve your goals for getting support.

Join a group of people in your area who can give you support and understanding in person. Many groups help people with different problems at places like hospitals and churches. Go to meetings often to meet people who have been through the same things as you. They can offer support, understanding, and helpful advice.

Join online groups and forums to meet people and share ideas from home: Join websites like Reddit, Facebook Groups, or forums about things you like. Join conversations, tell your story, and help others facing the same problems. Online communities let you meet people from all over the world who have similar interests or challenges, so you can learn from different points of view.

Participate actively and genuinely: Share your thoughts, feelings, and experiences honestly in the support group or online community. Share your difficulties and problems, as well as your accomplishments and victories, openly and truthfully. Help and encourage others who are going through the same tough times, and show them that you understand and care about their feelings. Creating real relationships and making people feel like they belong in the community can help them feel emotionally supported and validated.

Get help from others: Use the knowledge and experience of the group or online community to find advice, guidance, and resources to help you with your problems. Ask for help if you need it. Tell people how you feel and ask for advice on how to handle it. You can ask for ways to make yourself feel better or for support in dealing with your problems. Listen to what others have to say about how you're doing, and think about how it could help you get better and grow.

Set limits and keep personal information private when using support groups and online communities. It's important to protect your privacy and keep things confidential. Only tell people your personal information if you are okay with it and be careful about who can see it in the group or community. Take care of your mind and feelings by setting boundaries and taking breaks when you need to, so you don't get too overwhelmed or exhausted.

Think about getting help from a professional: Support groups and online communities are great for getting support and encouragement from people like you, but they are not the same as getting help from a professional. If you're having serious mental health problems for a long time, think about getting help from a mental health expert like a therapist, counselor, or psychiatrist. Professional help can be added to the help you get from friends and communities. It can include personalized treatment and therapy that is designed for your specific needs.

When you get help from a group or online community, think about helping others who are going through the same things. Help new people by sharing what you know and how you handle things. Also, support and encourage those who are having a hard time. By being helpful to the community, you not only make a difference to others but also feel good about yourself and connected to others.

Getting help from a group or online community can make you feel better and give you some strength when you're going through tough times. If you are struggling with mental health problems, ongoing illness, recovering from addiction, or other tough situations in life, talking to people who have been through similar things can help you feel like you belong and become stronger. Take the chance to connect with others, tell your story, and get support and encouragement as you work towards feeling better and getting stronger.

1. Do things that make you happy and have fun.

Doing things that make you happy and laughing a lot is not only fun but also important for keeping your mind healthy and happy. Science has shown that laughing is good for our bodies and minds. It can make us feel less stressed, happier, and healthier. Here are some ways to add more happiness and fun to your life:

Be with your friends and family who make you feel good and bring joy and laughter to your life. Organize events like parties, game nights, or movie marathons with people who make you happy and positive. Laughing together brings people closer and helps them feel like they belong together.

Spend time watching funny TV shows or movies that always make you laugh. Enjoy funny TV shows, comedy acts, or romantic comedies that make you laugh and feel happy. Laughter gets passed on easily, so ask others to come to laugh with you while watching a funny movie.

Have fun and play games to bring back the joy of being a kid again. You can have fun without worrying about what other people think or about your duties. You can play games, have water fights, or build sandcastles at the beach. Just enjoy yourself and have a good time. Being playful helps you be more creative, and spontaneous, and feel amazed.

Go see a fun comedy show or improv performance at a comedy club or theater. It will make you laugh and have a good time. Watching a funny comedy show or improv can make you feel happier and more energized. Ask your friends or family to come and laugh with you for a fun night.

Try different therapies like laughter yoga or laughter therapy. These involve doing exercises and techniques to make yourself laugh and feel happy. Go to laughter yoga classes or workshops where people do fun laughing exercises, deep breathing, and relaxing methods to help their bodies and emotions be healthier.

Tell funny stories or jokes to make your friends, coworkers, or acquaintances laugh and have a good time. Spread happiness Humor can help people feel more comfortable, relax in stressful situations, and make friendships stronger. Try to add some funny things to your conversations, like telling a joke or sharing a funny picture. It can make your interactions more enjoyable.

Develop your ability to find things funny. Look for the funny side of things in your daily life, even when things are tough. Approaching life with a fun and positive attitude can help you deal with hard times in a strong and hopeful way. Find the funny in strange, ironic, or odd things about people, and don't be afraid to laugh at yourself and your errors.

Be creative by writing, drawing, painting, or doing other artsy things that make you happy and let you use your imagination. Being creative and expressing yourself can make you feel really good and help you deal with stress and emotions. Give yourself the freedom to try new things without worrying about what others think, and concentrate on enjoying the activity instead of worrying about the final result.

Adding more laughter and happiness to your life can have a big impact on how you think and feel. Make sure to do things that make you happy, spend time with positive and funny people, and laugh a lot to make yourself feel better and have a happier life. Keep in mind that laughing is not just something that spreads from person to person, but it's also really helpful for being strong, building relationships, and enjoying the fun parts of life.

1. **Manage your time well and make self-reflection a priority.**

Within the hustle and haste of advanced life, time regularly feels like a rare asset, taking off small room for self-care and reflection. Be that as it may, prioritizing time administration and self-reflection is vital for keeping up ideal mental well-being. Here's why:

Decrease Push: Successful time administration can ease stretch by making a difference you prioritize assignments, set reasonable objectives, and make a sense of control over your plan. By apportioning time for self-care activities and unwinding, you'll prevent burnout and advance by and large well-being.

Improve Efficiency: Once you oversee your time well, you get to be more productive and beneficial in your everyday exercises. This permits you to achieve errands more successfully, clearing you with more time for self-reflection and exercises that feed your mental well-being.

Improve Decision-Making: Self-reflection gives profitable openings to delay, assess, and learn from your encounters. By making self-reflection a need, you'll be able to pick up clarity on your values, qualities, and regions for development, driving you to more educated and certain decision-making.

Advance Self-Awareness: Taking time for self-reflection permits you to tune into your considerations, sentiments, and behaviors. This increased self-awareness empowers you to recognize potential triggers for push or uneasiness, as well as recognize designs that will be ruining your mental well-being.

Foster Strength: Locks in normal self-reflection and builds passionate flexibility by empowering versatile adapting procedures and self-regulation procedures. By developing a more profound understanding of yourself and your responses to stressors, you'll explore challenges with more noteworthy ease and bounce back more successfully.

Joining time administration methods such as prioritizing assignments, setting boundaries, and assigning duties can make space in your plan for significant self-reflection. Whether it's through journaling, meditation, or basically taking calm minutes to check in with yourself, making self-reflection a need cultivates a more profound association to your inward world and underpins your travel toward made strides in mental well-being. Keep in mind, that contributing time to yourself isn't selfish, it's a basic viewpoint of self-care and well-being.

1. **Change negative thoughts and use positive words when speaking to yourself.**

Understand Negative Thinking: Pay attention to negative thoughts that make you feel unsure, worried, or sad. Pay attention to when you have bad thoughts about yourself, like being too hard on yourself, thinking the worst will happen, or assuming people are thinking bad things about you. Figure out why you're thinking these things and what's making you believe them. By paying attention to these negative thoughts that come automatically, you can start to question and change them.

Question what you believe: Think about the proof that supports or goes against negative thoughts. Ask yourself if there is any proof to support your negative beliefs, or if they are just guesses, mistakes, or things from the past. Search for different ways to understand or explain the situation, and think about how looking at things in a fair and sensible way could make you see things differently.

Practice changing your negative thoughts to more positive and realistic ones using cognitive restructuring techniques. First, figure out what kind of negative thoughts you're having, like thinking in extremes, making generalizations, or taking things too personally. Next, try to counter these misunderstandings by thinking of more fair and reasonable ideas that show the real complexity of the situation.

Create positive thoughts and sentences to replace negative thoughts and beliefs. Pick positive and motivating phrases that show what you believe in, what you are good at, and what you want to achieve, and keep saying them to yourself often. Use positive statements to help build a mindset of being kind to yourself, being strong, and believing in yourself. Remember how valuable and capable you are, even when things are tough.

Learn to be aware and accepting: Use mindfulness and acceptance to control bad thoughts and feelings. Focus on being in the moment and paying attention to your thoughts and feelings without judging or getting too attached. It's okay to recognize and accept bad thoughts and feelings for a short time instead of trying to push them away or ignore them. When you are kind and understanding to yourself, it can help you feel better and not let negative thoughts bother you as much.

Get help and advice: Talk to people you trust like friends, family, or therapists when you're struggling with bad thoughts. Talk to people who can understand and support you when you are having a hard time. Sometimes, just talking to someone you trust about how you feel and what you think can help you see things in a new way and find better ways to handle your thoughts and feelings.

Be nice to yourself and show compassion, especially when you're feeling down or things aren't going well. Take care of yourself the way you would take care of a friend going through the same thing. Be kind and understanding to yourself when you face difficulties and challenges, instead of being hard on yourself. Being kind to yourself when you have bad thoughts helps you to be strong and feel good.

Replacing negative thoughts with positive ones and talking positively to yourself can help you become stronger, more confident, and feel better emotionally. By noticing when you're thinking negative thoughts, asking if they're true, and replacing them with more positive thoughts, you can change how you see things and feel about life. Use these techniques every day to make your mind stronger and to have a better and kinder relationship with yourself.

1. **Do puzzles or play brain games often to keep your mind sharp.**

Keep Your Brain Active: Just like working out is important for staying healthy, doing activities that challenge your brain is important for keeping it sharp and quick. Doing mental exercises often can make your brain work better. It can help you remember things, pay attention, and solve problems. You can improve your brain's ability to change and learn new things by doing puzzles, games, and other mental activities.

Choose different activities: There are many puzzles and games to pick from, like crosswords, Sudoku, and jigsaw puzzles. There are also newer brain-training games and apps that focus on improving certain thinking skills. Try different activities to keep your brain sharp, like puzzles, memory games, and word games. This will help you think and problem-solve in different ways.

Include Learning and Creativity: Mental activities don't have to be just puzzles and games. They can include things that help you learn, be creative, and keep your mind sharp. Try learning something new like playing an instrument, learning a new language, or doing arts or crafts. It can be good for your brain. Doing creative things makes your brain work better and gives you a chance to express yourself and grow as a person.

Get into the habit: Doing mental exercises regularly is important to see results. Get in the habit of doing brain exercises regularly. Take time each day or week to work your brain and make it smarter. Add thinking activities to your everyday schedule, like doing a puzzle when you take a coffee break, playing a brain game on your phone while you travel, or joining a trivia game with friends once a week.

Push yourself to get the most out of mental exercise. It's important to challenge yourself and do things that are not easy for you. Pick things to do that are hard enough to make your brain work and help you get better and smarter as time goes on. Don't be scared to try hard puzzles or games that need you to think and problem-solve, because overcoming challenges helps make your mind stronger and more flexible.

Keep in touch with others: You can do mental activities like board games and card games with friends. Doing activities with other people is not only fun and makes you feel close to them, but it also helps you connect with others, which is important for your mental and emotional health. You should think about joining a book club, going to a game night, or joining a trivia competition in your area to have fun and meet new people while also keeping your brain active.

Keep an eye on how well you do as you do mental exercises regularly. Pay attention to any changes in how well you think, remember things, or solve problems as time goes by. Be happy about your accomplishments and important events in your life. Think about how keeping your brain active makes you feel better and have a better life. Use your improvement as a reason to keep trying new things that challenge your mind and help it grow.

Doing puzzles, playing brain games, and doing creative things can help keep your brain healthy as you get older. By keeping your brain active, trying new things, and staying connected with others, you can improve how your brain works and stay sharp as you get older. Make sure to do brain exercises every day. This will make your brain healthier and happier for a long time.

1. Establish limits and know when to refuse if needed.

It's important to know why boundaries are important. Boundaries help keep relationships healthy, protect your well-being, and make sure you have enough time, energy, and emotional strength for yourself. They show you what is okay and not okay when you interact with others, and help you feel good about yourself and make your own choices. Acknowledging that setting limits is not selfish but a way to take care of yourself and protect yourself.

Think about what you need and what is important to you. Figure out where you need to set limits in your life. Think about times when you feel like you have too much to do, or like you are really stressed out, or like you are mad at someone. Notice when people are not taking care of you or treating you well. Be honest with yourself about what you can handle and take care of yourself by setting boundaries to protect your health.

Tell people what your limits are in a nice and confident way. Say how you feel and what you need without blaming anyone else. Use "I" statements to express yourself. Be clear about what actions or behaviors are making you uncomfortable, and explain what will happen if they continue. Establish clear and steady limits in your relationships and use strong but polite communication to reinforce them.

Learn to say no without feeling bad or saying sorry when someone is crossing your boundaries or when you need to take care of yourself. Saying no doesn't mean rejecting others, it just means you're taking care of yourself and setting boundaries. Practice speaking up firmly and confidently, and if needed, give a short explanation for your decision. Stick to your choice and don't feel like you have to explain or defend it.

Listen to your gut feeling: When it comes to deciding and sticking to the rules in your relationships, trust your instincts and intuition. Be aware of how you feel and react in different situations, and pay attention to your inner feelings that tell you when someone is crossing your boundaries or when you need to stand up for yourself. Believe in yourself to make good choices and take care of yourself, even if it makes others unhappy.

Be consistent and firm: It is important to always stick to and enforce the rules you set. Be strong and stick to your limits, even if others try to persuade you otherwise. Don't break your rules or give in because you feel guilty or scared of arguments. Have self-respect and make sure you stick to your limits all the time. This is important for keeping your honesty and self-respect.

Ask for help when you need it: If you have trouble setting limits or making sure others follow them, talk to people you trust for help, like friends, family, or mental health experts. Surround yourself with people who understand and respect your limits, and ask for help from those who have been through the same tough times. Don't forget, you don't have to do boundary-setting by yourself. It's okay to ask for help, and it shows that you're strong, not weak.

Learning when to say no and setting limits is an important part of taking care of yourself and respecting yourself. Recognize what you need, tell people your limits, and stand up for yourself. This will help you have better relationships, take care of yourself, and live a life that fits with what's important to you. Keep in mind that boundaries help build strong and respectful relationships, they are not meant to separate people.

### 1.	Embrace your flaws and be okay with who you are.

Understand and appreciate the beauty of not being perfect: Embracing imperfection means recognizing and celebrating the special qualities that make you, you. Instead of trying to be perfect all the time, it's okay to embrace the beauty in our flaws and understand that it's normal to make mistakes. Know that your flaws make you more interesting and real to others because they show your unique qualities and make people like you more.

Stop expecting too much: Free yourself from the stress of trying to meet unrealistic goals, whether they come from society, media, or your own inner thoughts. Know that perfect is not real and trying to be perfect will make you feel bad and unsure of yourself. Instead, make achievable goals and standards for yourself, aiming for progress instead of being perfect. It's okay to make mistakes and learn from them as you go.

Be kind to yourself when you're having a hard time: Practice self-compassion and understand that it's okay to be gentle with yourself. Be kind and gentle to yourself, just like you would be to a friend going through a tough time. Be kind to yourself when you talk to yourself. Understand your feelings and experiences with kindness instead of being hard on yourself.

Pay attention to who you are on the inside and what is important to you: Stop looking only at how you look or what you have achieved, and start to think about your personality and what you believe in. That is what really shows your value and who you are. Understand that what really matters about you is how you act, if you are honest and good to others, and how strong you are, not just what you look like or what you have achieved. Build your confidence by knowing that you are valuable just for being yourself, without needing praise or approval from others.

Celebrate the things you are good at: Be proud of the things you are good at and the things you have achieved. Embrace the qualities that make you different from others. Understand that everyone is good at some things and not so good at others and that having different skills and abilities makes the world better. Be proud and confident in what you are good at. Know that it makes you special and important.

Be thankful and appreciative for the good things in your life, and accept both the good and tough times that happen to you. Practice being grateful for what you have. Understand that life has good and bad times and unexpected changes, and each thing you go through helps you become a better person. Enjoy the present moment and be grateful. Trust that you can handle life's challenges with strength and grace.

Find people who are kind and understanding, and who will accept you just the way you are, even with your imperfections. Find people and groups that make you feel important, welcomed, and understood. Be open and honest about who you are in those relationships. Seek comfort in the company of those who like your flaws and support you to be yourself without feeling sorry.

Accepting our flaws and learning to love ourselves is a journey that needs us to be patient, kind, and brave. By not expecting too much from yourself, accepting and being proud of the things that make you different, and celebrating what you're good at, you can learn to love and appreciate yourself for who you are, even if you're not perfect. Don't worry about being perfect. Be happy by being yourself and living your life with joy, purpose, and self-love.

Secret Nugget: Acupuncture Points for Stress Relief and Pain Management

I really appreciate you for reading up until this point and I added these additional nuggets of info regarding some exercises you can do to improve your daily life without needing to pay someone else!

In alternative medicine, acupuncture is highly respected for its ability to reduce stress and ease pain. But, not many people know that choosing the right acupuncture points can make the benefits even better.

In traditional acupuncture, specific points on the body are targeted to treat different health problems. Some of these points are designed to specifically help with stress and pain relief. These points are called "stress-relief" points and can be activated with acupuncture or acupressure.

In addition to acupuncture, doing specific exercises can make stress relief and pain management work even better. These exercises like *qigong, tai chi,* and yoga, work together with acupuncture to help balance the body's energy system called *Qi.*

A really good exercise is called "*Eight Brocades*" qigong. It includes gentle movements while doing deep breathing at the same time. This helps the body's energy flow better and also makes you feel more relaxed and clear-minded.

Another helpful exercise is called "*Mindful Movement Yoga,*" which includes regular yoga poses along with techniques to be more aware and focused. This method not only helps reduce tension in the body but also helps strengthen the mind, making it a great addition to acupuncture therapy.

You can use acupuncture points and exercises to help reduce stress and pain and improve your overall mental health and well-being.

Don't forget, that finding good mental health involves many different things, like trying acupuncture and doing mindful exercises. These things can help you feel a lot better and make big changes in your life.

I hope you find mental wellness through old healing methods and taking care of your whole self.

Finally the last nugget, (*I PROMISE*)

Another piece of my passion is creating and inspiring sustainability that changes the way we treat the world we take for granted daily. If you don't know anything about solar energy, here you go...

Revealing the Secret Strength of Sun Power

In the search for energy that is good for the environment, solar power is a great option. But we don't know exactly how much it can help yet.

In addition to helping the environment and saving money on energy, there are other things about solar power that could change the way we think about and use the sun's energy.

There's a lot of solar energy. In one hour, the sun gives enough energy to power the whole world for a year.

But we're only using a little bit of this huge energy. By using solar technology, we can use a lot of clean energy that could change how we power our world.

Living off-grid means being independent from the main electricity system. Many people think that only city-dwellers connected to the main power grid can use solar energy, but that's not true.

People who live in remote areas without access to electricity can use solar power systems.

They don't need a lot of infrastructure to get reliable electricity. Imagine how much better it would be if we could use solar power to bring electricity to faraway villages or places that have been hit by disasters.

It's not just for rooftop panels or big solar farms. New solar technology has led to many new ways to use it, like making saltwater drinkable with solar power, and using solar power to charge electronic devices on the go.

These new ideas help more people use clean energy and also help businesses grow and stay strong in different industries.

Solar energy is very strong and reliable, especially in bad weather or if the power grid stops working.

Solar-powered homes can keep working even when the power goes out if they have good storage systems like batteries.

This means they can stay on when regular power goes out and keep providing electricity.

Solar energy not only helps reduce carbon emissions, but it also has other good effects on the environment that people don't always talk about.

By using solar power, we use less coal, oil, and natural gas. This helps protect the environment and save important habitats.

The solar industry does more than just help the planet; it also helps people find work and makes the economy stronger.

The solar industry provides many jobs that help local economies and the world. These jobs include making and installing solar panels, as well as researching and developing new solar technology.

Solar energy gives people and communities the power to control their own energy future, creating a more spread out energy system called energy democracy. Solar technology allows ordinary people, businesses, and neighborhoods to take part in creating sustainable energy for the future.

I do want to disclose that on a side note, I also sell solar however the point of this information is not to sell you anything but rather provide knowledge to the uninformed.

There are too many predatory practices involving solar energy that it isn't even funny.

I am here to provide as much value and knowledge as I can for little to no cost to you!

If you're still looking for more information, you can find it on my website:

MarquiseTheCoach.com[1]

Congrats! You reached the actual end!

Thank you for embarking on this journey to nurture your mental health with me. Remember, mental health is not a destination but a daily practice.

Each day presents an opportunity for growth, healing, and self-discovery.

If you're eager to continue your journey or seek further guidance on enhancing your mental well-being, visit the website where I also have my podcast called Only Humble Motives(OHM) and i even have an episode where i give some affirmations to speak love into your life!

My vision for this movement is to inspire awareness of ourselves and how internal/external factors greatly affect our daily lives and overall being.

Together, let's commit to prioritizing our mental health, one small step at a time. Because every effort we make today contributes to a brighter, healthier tomorrow.

With gratitude,

Marquise The Coach

---

1. http://marqusisethecoach.com

Don't miss out!

Visit the website below and you can sign up to receive emails whenever Marquise The Coach publishes a new book. There's no charge and no obligation.

https://books2read.com/r/B-A-QBWDB-QTJZC

BOOKS2READ

Connecting independent readers to independent writers.

MARQUISE

About the Author

As an author, coach, and advocate for holistic living, Marquise is on a mission to change lives—one mindset at a time. With a passion for inspiring mindfulness, awareness, and sustainable living, Marquise's journey is deeply rooted in a commitment to personal growth and societal well-being.

From a young age, Marquise felt called to make a positive impact on the world, driven by a profound sense of empathy and compassion for others. This innate desire led Marquise to pursue a path dedicated to understanding the complexities of the human mind and exploring innovative approaches to fostering well-being.

With years of experience as a coach and mentor, Marquise has witnessed firsthand the transformative power of mindfulness and awareness. By guiding individuals to cultivate a deeper connection with themselves and the world around them, Marquise empowers others to live authentically and consciously, making choices aligned with their values and aspirations.

In addition to promoting personal growth, Marquise is deeply passionate about sustainable living and environmental stewardship.

Recognizing the interconnectedness of all living beings and the planet we call home, Marquise advocates for mindful consumption, eco-friendly practices, and conscious living habits that honor the Earth and support future generations.

Through Marquise's writing, coaching, and advocacy efforts, countless individuals have found inspiration, guidance, and empowerment on their journey toward a more fulfilling and sustainable way of life. With unwavering dedication and a heart full of compassion, Marquise continues to make a difference in the world, one mindset at a time.

Read more at https://marquisethecoach.com/.

www.ingramcontent.com/pod-product-compliance
Lightning Source LLC
Chambersburg PA
CBHW031441130726
47989CB00003B/1239